Off to a
Good Start

Launching the
School Year

#1 · THE RESPONSIVE CLASSROOM SERIES ·

Excerpts from the
Responsive Classroom Newsletter

Northeast Foundation for Children

SINCE 1981

All net proceeds from the sale of *Off to a Good Start: Launching the School Year* support the work of Northeast Foundation for Children, Inc., a nonprofit, educational foundation established to demonstrate through teaching, research and consultation a sensible and systematic approach to schooling.

ISBN 0-9618636-6-8
Library of Congress catalog card number 97-68711

Second printing August 1998

Photographs: Marlynn Clayton, Timothy Coleman, William Elwell, Glenn Morin, Peter Wrenn, Cherry Wyman

Cover and book design: Woodward Design

Northeast Foundation for Children
71 Montague City Road
Greenfield, MA 01301
1-800-360-6332

Table of Contents

The First Six Weeks of School
Building the Foundation
for a Successful Year

by Ruth S. Charney and Marlynn K. Clayton

O VER THE YEARS our teaching experience has taught us how critical the first weeks of school are to the success of the entire year. What follows is our framework for creating an environment in which children can be academically and socially successful. Please keep in mind that this is not a recipe set in stone, but that you, as teachers, must try it out and make it work for you.

A Responsive Classroom brings together an academic curriculum based on developmentally appropriate practices and a social curriculum that builds a caring, respectful community. Establishing such a classroom during the beginning weeks of school must be a slow and deliberate process. It involves several strategies and phases that delicately balance the emphasis between academic and social goals.

The "Social Curriculum"

The focus of the social curriculum for these first six weeks is ethical behavior, classroom management and group building. In respectful and proactive ways, children are taught expectations for behavior, care for themselves, each other and their materials and the skills necessary to be independent and motivated learners.

Children are involved in the process in such a way that they feel an ownership and responsibility for the management and ethical behavior that is established.

The academic curriculum is gradually introduced in these first six weeks, while the social curriculum is emphasized. Children use their academic skills in activities that lead to group building, care of the learning environment, and exploration of the possibilities for future learning.

Children are thus given the opportunity to begin the year feeling confident about academic skills in non-threatening ways before plunging into new academic work. Teachers have the opportunity to observe children's present knowledge and skills as they are applied in an integrated fashion.

Frequent whole group activities are important in the first week of school.

Week 1

During the first week of school, three strategies will be used:

Building a Sense of Group,

Establishing Rules and

Guided Discovery.

Building a Sense of Group includes: establishing a *Morning Meeting* ritual (Greeting, Activity, News and Announcements, Rules), establishing *Sharing* (what happened in school today) and *Representing* (sharing of work done in school) times, and doing lots of whole group activities for both inside and outside that are non-competitive and help children get to know each other and work together. Include simple activities that help the group to take ownership of their learning environment (i.e. bulletin boards, labels, organization of materials, etc.).

Establishing Rules requires having an initial discussion of classroom goals with the students. Rules should be *explored* and generated with the students and gradually set in place.

The teacher should make no assumptions, but should teach, model, role play and practice expected behaviors for classroom routines, lunch, recess, bathroom, halls, specials, etc. This will also be the time to teach and practice management signals, such as a bell or hands-up.

The third strategy, *Guided Discovery,* is a method by which areas of the room or classroom materials are introduced slowly and deliberately to the whole class. Rules and expectations are carefully established for the use of these materials or areas. Initially, very few materials are on the shelves and a limited number of areas of the room are open. You'll find that children are excited and motivated to use the materials or areas as they are opened through the *Guided Discovery.*

The easiest areas are introduced first, as are the materials that children probably have some prior knowledge about or are very simple and/or open-ended in their use. For example, in the art center, the only materials available might be crayons, paper and pencils; in the library, start with only a few more books than the number of children in the room; in the math area, have only one manipulative to start, with plenty of time to explore.

Teachers must be sure that there is a balance of outside and inside time, quiet and active times and whole group and smaller group times during the day in order to meet the developmental needs of each age.

These first three strategies are alternated throughout the day all during the first week. When enough materials/areas have been introduced so that all the children can work in small groups with different materials or activities, and the children respond well to the management signals, then the fourth strategy is added.

Activity Time is the precursor to *Choice Time* and *Single-Topic Choice.* During *Activity Time* children work in assigned areas or activities for a 15–30 minute period, depending on the age of the

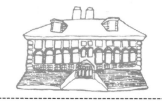
children, while the teacher has the opportunity to observe and reinforce appropriate behaviors modeled in the *Guided Discoveries*.

For example, one group might be working with clay, another with a game and another with drawing materials. The teacher should use this time to practice the 3 R's of proactive discipline: *Reinforce, Remind and Redirect*.

The *Activity Time* also gives the teacher the opportunity to introduce the idea of *"Have-to's"* (teacher-directed work) and to extend *Representing*.

Week 2

In the second week, the teacher will want to continue with the same strategies as in the first week. The teacher should interact with children in all parts of the room and continue to make the children feel that he/she is everywhere and seeing everything by doing the 3 R's.

Activity Time should be introduced, if it wasn't already begun during the first week. If it was introduced last week, it may be possible to increase the length of activity time or to add another to the day's schedule.

Also this week, *Sharing* can be taught during *Morning Meeting,* if the children show that they can manage listening well enough.

4

Students learn where different materials belong
and how to care for them.

The list of rules should be finished and posted for all children to see at all times. Make time every day for short role plays to examine rules and practice appropriate behaviors. Begin to explore *Logical Consequences* with the class through discussion and modeling.

Introduce new areas and materials once the children show good use of materials that have already been introduced. When enough materials/areas have been introduced so that every child can make a "real choice" of an activity (several more choices available for children to choose from than there are children in the class) and the children have shown that they can manage themselves and the materials in an *Activity Time,* then the group is ready to learn about and practice *Choice Time* or *Single-Topic Choice.*

Choice Time begins with a half-hour period at a time. Children choose verbally and the teacher records the choices on a chart, or children can sign up or hang up names under listed choices. The teacher should move from area to area, as an observer, facilitator and namer of behavior, using the 3 R's: *Reinforce, Remind, Refocus*. The teacher makes time each day for some children to "represent" work done during *Choice Time*.

For *Single-Topic Choice,* begin with a simple topic that will allow every child to experience mastery. For example, the students could each choose a way to show their favorite part of the book currently being read aloud.

Excellent ideas for *Single-Topic Choice* in the first few weeks include those that help to build group identity and cohesion. For example, every child could choose a way to tell about a favorite interest, or a summer experience. Children could work in partners and after doing interviews of their partner, choose a way to share what they learned about their partner.

Week 3

It is still important to continue with all previous strategies this week. Continue to role play by practicing expected behaviors. An understanding of *Logical Consequences* should be established by the end of the week.

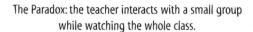

The Paradox: the teacher interacts with a small group while watching the whole class.

During the third week, it may be time to introduce *The Paradox*. The teacher begins to take a small group of children for group work, while the rest of the class is having a *Choice Time*. While the children think that the teacher is totally involved with the small group, the teacher is really watching the whole class very carefully and doing the 3 R's from where she/he is.

The small group should work on something that takes little teacher input or direction so that the majority of the teacher's attention can actually be directed to the actions of the rest of the class. Children will learn to manage themselves while the teacher is involved in the small group work. Children in this small group must have *Choice* at another time of the day.

This week re-introduce the concept of *Have-To's* (teacher assigned work). When children gather for small group work it is named a *Have-To*.

Teach, model, role play and practice what to do when the teacher is involved with a small group. Now is the time that the children begin to see themselves as peer teachers.

Week 4

The fourth week is really a continuation of all the activities and strategies that have been introduced over the past three weeks. Increasing attention can be paid to small group work, while still doing *The Paradox*.

This is a good time to introduce science or blocks, which need more teacher input and direction in the *Guided Discovery*, as a small group activity.

Week 5

During the fifth week the teacher should continue with activities and strategies of the past four weeks, especially remembering group building games and activities.

The teacher should now be able to give increased attention to small group work. Written planning for *Choice Time* or *Single-Topic Choice* could be introduced in small group time, if not previously done.

Week 6

Finally, in the sixth week, it's time to begin the teaching that demands the teacher's most intense attention, in small group reading, math and other curriculum areas, while the activities and strategies of the past five weeks continue.

Each day should have a balance of whole group activity, small group activity and individual attention for each child. Each day should also have a balance of teacher-directed work *(Have-To's)* and child-initiated work. Each should carry equal value in the classroom.

The Foundation Is Now in Place

The first six weeks have now been completed, and the foundation has been established. The class should now manage quite smoothly. However, the teacher must continue to give "management tune-ups" throughout the year, especially after vacations and long weekends.

Management issues are a normal part of classroom life. When management is taught in this way, children are capable of taking an active role in finding solutions that work!

One very important consideration to keep in mind is that each group of children is unique and will move at their own rate. Some groups will be ready for *The Paradox* in Week 2 and others won't be ready until Week 3 or even Week 4.

Older children in particular, who have never had the opportunity to make real choices in their classrooms before, will need more time to adjust and learn how to handle themselves responsibly.

Be Nice!
and Other Classroom Rules
Creating a Caring Community with Children
by Ruth S. Charney

CREATING RULES with children is an important part of the first six weeks of school. These rules help set the classroom tone for the year. I have found children are more apt to respect rules they help make, and that rules lead to greater growth if they are framed in the positive. I know that classrooms are happier with a few rules that are honored than many rules that are forgotten.

Making the Rules

"We are all workers in school," I tell the children. "What are the most important rules we need to help us in our work?" Discussions follow, discussions that help move children from the most narrow self-interest to collective ideas of fairness and consideration. We work on rules for our games and rules for our classroom. Setting up rules may involve a lengthy process of construction, with the children taking much of the responsibility. Or the teacher may simply suggest rules that the children amend or put into their own words. Both methods work if children are given a voice and an opportunity to explore the meaning of rules before they are adopted.

Some Guidelines

Rules provide positive directions—what you do, not what you don't do.

Rules serve a purpose. The purpose is to make our classrooms and school a good and safe place for teachers and children. For example, it's hard to do good work if you fear mistakes. So a good rule might be that people offer constructive comments about others' work and not laugh.

Rules need to be meaningful to the workplace and the workers. This means specific and concrete. We need to know when we are following a rule and when we are not.

Few is better than many. Rules should be posted and easy to read.

Below I elaborate an example of the rule-making process that occurred in a fifth grade class. Although it served as an introduction to a social studies unit, it is used here as an illustration of one approach to beginning the rule-making process during the first six weeks of school. Its basic lessons apply to all grade levels, although its thoroughness is appropriate for the middle and upper grades. There are many ways to conduct rule-setting sessions with students. It is important to remember that the process is a collaboration. Teachers are not turning over the task, nor do we lead students to foregone conclusions.

A Fifth Grade Charter

When I decided to construct a classroom "constitution" with a fifth grade class to initiate a unit of the American Revolution, the construction process quickly expanded. It became much more important and useful than any single social studies unit.

"Tell me any rules you know," I began, although I might have gotten a truer response had I asked them to tell me all the rules they broke in a week's time!

"You mean like no chewin' gum in school?" Alex's cheek puffed with a wad of gum pocketed in one side.

"Yes. Like that."

"No running in the hallways."

"No fighting."

"No swears."

"No taking someone's money or stuff."

"Be nice."

"That's not a rule!" someone protested.

Students tally results from classmates' rule sheets.

I wrote "Be nice!" on the chart headed "Rules." I wrote down all the rules they said, which numbered close to fifty. Most began with "no." I told them to think about it and to add any more rules they remembered before the next day.

I transcribed the chart for the next day's meeting and I gave everyone a copy. "Check the rules you like. Cross out the rules you don't like."

"Whattaya' mean?"

"Some of these rules you like. You might say to yourself, 'That's a good rule.' Some rules may seem silly or not important or even wrong. Cross those out."

"Most rules are dumb 'cause nobody can make you do stuff," Roger stated.

"You mean if you don't follow a rule, it's a bad rule?"

"Yeah."

"Okay, but for now imagine what rules you might make yourself follow if you could boss yourself."

Roger nodded.

I incorporated Roger's idea and suggested that we add a new notation. "If you like a rule, but think it's hard to follow put a star beside it."

When I collected their rule-sheets, I was struck with the clear patterns and common themes. Rules about safety were checked as "liked." Rules about personal styles (gum chewing, candy, dress codes, swearing) were often crossed out. Rules about ethics and "rights of others" (stealing, fighting, cheating, name-calling) were good rules but qualified by the stars—hard to follow. Rules concerning classroom conduct were also starred—no talking, quiet voices, don't bother or interrupt, stay in our seat, etc. There were more stars or checks than cross-outs, even from this band of rule-shakers!

For the next meeting, I returned their rule-sheets so that we could examine the results together. I assigned everyone in the class a job—to collect information, collate the responses and report on the data. Children cut their rule-sheets into strips, passed them out and then tallied their slips. We gathered again when everyone had checked and rechecked their figures. Considerable interest and investment in the survey were building. They were excited about discovering the group reactions and regarding themselves as researchers.

The group was quiet, almost solemn, as students presented their reports. One student entered the information on a master list. Sometimes I interrupted and asked for predictions, but mostly the children were intent on finding out, item by item. Towards the end, however, children were seeing patterns and spontaneously drawing conclusions. Despite the momentum, I postponed further discussion for the next day and gave out a second worksheet with questions to help them begin to organize and classify the information.

1. What are the most popular rules?

Fifth and sixth graders made this poster to illustrate
their rules for meetings.

2. What rules were least liked by the class?

3. What kinds of rules did people like/not like?

4. What kinds of rules had stars?

5. What do you think would be the most important rules, if
   you could only choose one of these?

Immediately students asked what I meant by "kinds of rules."

I explained that I wanted them to think about how some of the rules were similar or different and might be grouped together. "Are some rules easy, and that's why people like them? Picking up trash is easy. Not fighting is hard. Do kids like easy rules and not like hard ones?" I pointed out they were now trying to understand and interpret the research they had gathered.

There was a clear agreement on counting the checks or crossouts. But controversy surrounded the starred items. "Be nice"—one girl pointed out—was the most popular, if you counted the checks and the stars.

Children also noted the popularity of categories that included ideas of safety, care and fairness. Someone else had come up with two categories, "kid rules" and "teacher rules." Kid rules were rules that kids needed and teacher rules were the ones the teachers wanted. Roger had stayed with his enforcement concerns and divided rules according to how you might get caught, in which he raised issues of intrinsic moral conflicts as well as external sanctions. "If you cheat and no one catches you, or if you fight outside of school..."

The most vigorous discussion centered on question five, the "most important rule," although just as we got into it, something else occurred. I stopped reminding and monitoring the interruptions, and the rule about raising hands in a meeting was quickly lost in the excitement. I had stopped "enforcement," as Roger would say. The tone of the meeting changed to a more competitive and edgy one.

"Hey, I was talking and you butted in."

"Yeah. But you've been saying and saying." Chuckles. Hand slaps.

"Teacher, don't people got to raise their hands?"

"Why?"

"It's a rule."

"So?"

"So, if it's a rule, people got to do it."

"But you listed over fifty rules and a lot of them you don't like, a lot are hard and many you don't even try to do. So what's a rule?"

There was a connection forming between needs and the concept of rules. Again I asked them to choose one rule that they thought would be most important for our classroom this year. I said that they could combine or reword the rules from our charts. I added one more thumbprint. I said that I didn't like rules that began with "no" and that they needed to state their rules in a "yes." I reminded them that they had already figured a lot of this out. They liked rules that kept people safe; they liked rules that involved being nice to each other; they liked rules that had to do with fairness.

The aim was for everyone to contribute a rule he or she agreed was important to create our class charter. To avoid a long list we combined and honed until there were six:

1. We will treat each other fairly.

2. We will keep quiet when others are working.

3. We will help teachers or classmates when they ask for help.

4. We will walk in the halls and in the classroom.

5. We will try to solve disagreements by talking it over ourselves. If we can't, we will ask the teacher to help us.

6. We will use only the things we need and put the tops back on stuff.

Not all of these rules worked—or could work—but it was a powerful beginning and instilled a sense of mutual responsibility. The interest of these students in ethical issues was keen and incontestable, even if there were moments when it was more to someone's advantage to exploit others than to be fair!

The charter, and the standards the students had helped to create, had weight. From September to June the continuing conversations which engaged everyone in issues of right and wrong, good and bad rules, fair and not fair, added to the importance and the vigor of the document. I am certain that the charter would have failed without this on-going commitment to dialogue. "Amendments," we called it.

Eventually these fifth graders studied the United States Constitution. I recall Roger's brash pronouncement, "Hey, they did like us!"

Rules Grow from Our
Hopes and Dreams

by Marlynn K. Clayton and Chip Wood

THE RULES IN THE RESPONSIVE CLASSROOM should grow directly from the hopes and dreams of students and teachers. Hopes and dreams provide the intrinsic motivation for students to care for themselves, others, and their environment in ways that encourage each student to stretch and grow. The process of creating, interpreting and practicing rules gives students the opportunity to face some of the ethical complexities they will deal with throughout their lives.

Generating rules with students is not a new idea for many teachers. However, involving students in a process that begins with the assessment of hopes and dreams can be a powerful avenue to creating a caring classroom community through personal investment.

Sometimes, rules begin as a long list of negatives: "Don't run. Don't hit. Don't sharpen pencils while the teacher is talking. Don't eat in class." The rules go on and on until even the teacher can't remember them. Children often assume that if there's not a specific rule against an action, they're free to try it—"Teacher didn't say I couldn't play Power Rangers® at the science table."

In the Responsive Classroom, we suggest going through a conscious process with children at the beginning of each year to create a set of simple rules which guide all school behavior. Each class works on three to five rules which are:

Positive: guiding desired behavior rather than prohibiting negative behavior

Global: serving as broad guidelines for all types of situations

Constantly examined and interpreted: by students and teacher to fit specific situations

Creating the Rules

Creating classroom rules is an important task in the first days of school. The process sets a tone of collaboration and allows students to become strongly invested in rules and expectations.

Before the first day of class, teachers need to reflect on their own goals and dreams for the coming year—what they want most for the children in their classes. These goals help provide shape, structure and inspiration for the year's work.

In kindergarten and first grade, a tour of the room sparks questions about some of the activities that will be going on during the year. Just enough supplies are displayed to give the children ideas, but no more than the teacher will be able to introduce during the first week: the block area with a sign, "Opening Soon;" the painting easel without paints or paper yet; a sampling of books in the library; a couple of manipulatives on the manipulative shelf; crayons, pencils and markers on the art shelf. After each tour, the class meets to share some ideas about what might happen in the room.

After the class generates some ideas about their classroom, the teacher can add some personal ideas, and then lead the class toward an essential question. "One hope that I have is that you will be able to do the things that you most want to do in school this year. You have many wonderful ideas. What is it that you most hope to do in school this year?" The teacher then records each child's hope.

A chart might include:

Leon hopes to be able to climb on the outside climber.
Mary hopes to be able to play in the blocks.
Jeremy hopes he can have a friend.

It may take two or three days to share everyone's hopes, making sure that everyone is heard and recognized for a special hope. These may be reviewed with games, such as "Who can remember what Mary hopes she'll be able to do?" For older primary children the process might include a homework assignment to write and draw about their most important hope for this year.

Teachers can then share a condensed version of their hopes. "What I hope for most this year is that everyone will feel good and safe in school, that all students will reach their hopes, and that everyone will be a thinking worker." Discussion continues on what it means for people to feel "good" and "safe" and what a "thinking worker" is.

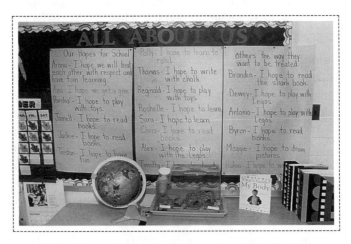

Children's hopes for the school year are prominently displayed.

The first bulletin board displays "Our Most Important Hopes and Dreams for This Year." Each child's works are displayed in beautiful writing accompanied by each child's drawing showing the child doing a special hope (and may include a photo of the child as well).

When the teacher's and students' hopes have been recognized and acknowledged, the class is ready to consider rules which serve them as individuals and as a community.

For older children (grades 4, 5 and 6) who are more familiar with rules and routines the process is the same, but the first bulletin board might exhibit the results of a homework assignment on individual goals. The goals can be shared in a meeting, with the teacher's input as well, and then all are displayed, as they were in Elizabeth Baker's fifth grade class in Washington, DC under the heading "Great Expectations."

Carefully planned meetings can help a class move from dreams and goals to rules which help those dreams come true. The class collaborates to form rules which protect and promote their dreams. For older children, a meeting might begin with a statement like this: "If these are our hopes and our dreams, what do you suppose are the rules we will need in our classroom in order to make these hopes and dreams come true?" For younger children, "How can we take care of ourselves and each other so that we can all do what we hope to do?" As ideas are shared, the teacher revisits the hopes to make the connection concrete.

First responses are nearly always expressed negatively, describing things that shouldn't happen—"Don't fight. Don't hit. Don't interrupt." After listing all of these, the teacher works with

Rules which emerged from class discussion are copied on a large poster.

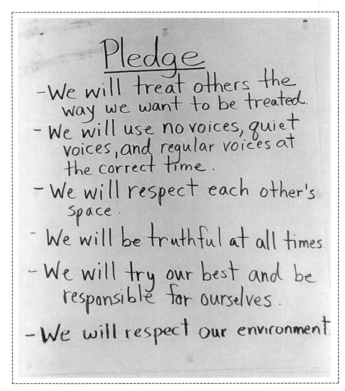

Pledge
- We will treat others the way we want to be treated.
- We will use no voices, quiet voices, and regular voices at the correct time.
- We will respect each other's space.
- We will be truthful at all times.
- We will try our best and be responsible for ourselves.
- We will respect our environment

the class to combine rules on similar subjects into general rules which are stated positively. This is not an easy process and may take considerable time, modeling and practice. "If we are not going to fight, what are we going to do when we want to resolve a conflict?"

The goal is to involve everyone in a process which creates three to five rules. The language will vary from class to class, but classroom rules cover three general categories:

Respect yourself.
Respect others.
Respect our environment.

An example from a fifth grade class is:

"We take care of our classroom. We help each other. We take care of ourselves."

The rules may then be copied to a large and beautiful poster and displayed along with each child's signature of agreement. Creating and listing positive, global rules doesn't guarantee that children truly understand them or are able to follow them. Additional steps are necessary.

Modeling the Rules

Class discussions about rules are the place to start, always referring back to the individual and community hopes and dreams. "How will we take care of ourselves around the climber so that Leon's hope will come true?" However, talking to children is not enough. It is very important for children in all grades to get chances to practice following and interpreting the rules through action.

Each classroom area may need attention, such as "How will we take care of our classroom when we are finished in the block area?" or "How will you help others who are in the library reading?" or "What might be friendly, caring things to say to others who are working with you at the art table?"

In each situation, children act out and then practice their ideas. Concrete examples and role-playing make the rules come alive and help children understand how actions build toward achievement for themselves and others in the class.

Supporting the Rules

Once the rules are posted and children have had a chance to discuss and practice them, the rules become guidelines for behavior in all types of situations.

By paying attention to the small positive behaviors, we encourage children to continue building those skills. By paying attention to the small negative behaviors, we catch those behaviors before a child is out of control, scared and threatened.

We focus on *the 3 R's—Reinforcing, Reminding and Redirecting. Reinforcing* means consistently using language that notices and supports children's positive behaviors.

Reinforcing becomes a habit and uses both language and non-verbal cues to help children recognize and continue their positive behavior. "Aaron, I notice that you are sharing with Jeremy." "Samuel, I noticed that you helped Brian at the computer this morning. Thank you." "Sarah, I appreciate the fact that you lined up quickly like we talked about. It will make our field trip easier."

Reinforcement is given directly to the children, rather than talking about them or using them to make others behave appropriately. It's best to use language of encouragement (which focuses on positive behavior) as opposed to language of praise (which focuses on the individual). We want children to work on behaving well for the intrinsic reasons connected with the positive behavior and not for a teacher's external praise.

Reminding focuses on the teacher's belief that children are capable of remembering and enacting positive behaviors. They are asked to remember the rules themselves and to make an interpretation which governs the specific situation, such as: "Lisa, show me how we take care of our paint supplies when we're done," or "Is there someone who can remind me what it means when I raise my hand in the classroom?"

Redirecting continues to focus on the rules but allows for no negotiation or interpretation. The message is, "I don't like what you're doing right now, but I do like you." Redirecting statements might include: "You need to go back to the edge of the playground and walk to the door again," or "Aaron, you need to do your writing without talking now."

Rules Support Hopes and Dreams

Rules in the Responsive Classroom are logical, positive outgrowths of the dreams and goals of students and teachers. They allow children to feel safe to take the necessary risks to learn, to help and respect others, and to care for their learning environment.

Because the rules are global rather than narrow and specific, children become skilled at interpreting guidelines rather than becoming restricted to "the letter of the law." The teacher's emphasis on the process of creating rules provides a strong reference point throughout the year. Teachers can direct all behavior and classroom activity toward what every child wants—achieving hopes and dreams.

Children's signatures indicate their agreement with this document expressing rules they generated.

From *Teaching Children to Care*
(by Ruth Sidney Charney, published by NEFC)

Creating rules with children is an important part of the work of the first six weeks of school. These rules help set the classroom tone for the year. I have found children are more apt to respect rules they help make, and I know that classrooms are happier with a few rules that are honored than many rules that are forgotten.

I do not want my rules to legislate every action. I want them to encourage reasoned thinking and discussion. I want rules that we "like," not because they give license or permission, but because they help us construct a community that is orderly and safe.

In the Greenfield Center School, the "Golden Rule" provides a unifying school ethic or principle. We call it our "one rule." It is certainly our first rule. [Each school can and should find the unifying rule that works best for its community and culture.] We explain that the Golden Rule is the ideal. It describes how we want to be with each other and how we want to be as a school.

"The Golden Rule," one 8 year old says, "means you gotta treat others as you want to be treated back." It directs us toward ideas of caring, but these ideas need to be anchored in particular actions and events for children to understand them.

The Golden Rule is introduced and practiced during the first six weeks of school. Children put it into their own words, write it out and post it in the room. It is a rule that governs by its repeated use, not by a single instance, and it can be applied to nearly every action of significance to children.

We desperately need to prepare children to examine questions of right and wrong for themselves and to see the consequences of their choices. The Golden Rule provides an ethical or moral reference point, a place to begin the search for different ways to act.

Activities for Building Community in Your Classroom

by Marlynn K. Clayton

R ESPONSIVE CLASSROOM teachers begin their school year with curriculum activities that build on their students' academic skills while at the same time creating a sense of community and class identity.

These curriculum activities require children to plan and problem solve, to express themselves in many different ways and media, to use their writing, reading and math skills, to actively listen, and to begin to build important social skills such as cooperation, assertion, responsibility, empathy and self-control.

They also provide critical opportunities for children to learn each other's names, interests, abilities and other personal information; to feel a sense of belonging; and to invest in caring about a group of people. The following activities are just a few ideas that have been used successfully over the years by teachers in many different Responsive Classroom settings and grade levels.

"Getting to Know One Another" Projects

Names

All students make name tags the first day and decorate them in a way that tells something about themselves. The name tags are shared with the rest of the class and are worn for at least the next 10 days. The name tags can also be made in duplicate and then used for drawing partners or determining who is to be greeted.

Community Building Activities

• During the next few days names are studied. Each child shares special information about his/her name—Does it have meaning? Where did it come from? Does it have a nickname or a short way to say it? Which way does he or she prefer?

- Children make a "name" bulletin board display with their name tags or with beautiful large writing in paint or markers.

- Children each create a name poster with fancy large letters going down the left hand side and descriptors about them going horizontally out from each letter.

SMART

AWESOME

MIGHTY

Once children know each other they can make a name poster for another class member.

Displaying students' self portraits helps give a sense of class identity.

Autobiographies

Children create autobiographies that tell about themselves. Based on age level, these autobiographies can be dictated, written and drawn. Beginning questions or topics to be answered can be presented by the teacher in ditto or photocopied format. Later, pages with children's questions can be added. These books include a self-portrait and sometimes photographs taken at school and/or from home.

Community Building Activities

- Children read and share their autobiographies with the whole class.

- Autobiographies are put into the class library.

- *Who am I?* A team of children prepare a series of bio sketches based on information gathered from the autobiographies. These sketches are presented in oral or dramatic form to the rest of the class who have to guess the name of the classmate being described.

- *Class Riddles*, based on shared autobiography information, are prepared by the teacher first and then later by the children. These riddles are written on the Morning Meeting message or presented at a Morning Meeting. They can be collected and put into book format for continued enjoyment and additions.

- *Bingo:* Teacher (or later a group of students) makes a bingo-type grid on a piece of paper. Into each square of the grid is put a piece of information that would apply to several or many of the children in the class (has a brother, went to the beach for vacation, ate spaghetti this week, etc.).

This sheet is photocopied so that every child has the same one. The object of the game is to walk around, ask each other questions based on the information in the grids, make an X on the squares when the information applies to the child asked and get three or four in a row or fill in a whole sheet (whatever rules have been established before starting).

One important rule is that each child may only ask one question of another child at a time and then has to move on to another child before coming back to the first child. It's great fun—particularly with older children and adults—and gets everyone laughing and talking with one another.

- *Pride Day:* Children write or dictate about something they can do that they are very proud of—sharing why this makes them proud and what they had to do to become so proud. Then each child has a scheduled day and time when they represent to the class by actually doing the activity. These events are recorded in photographs and tape recordings and displayed along with the child's explanation on a bulletin board and/or in a book.

Student partners interview each other, asking questions the class devised together.

Interviews

Children are partnered with someone they do not know very well and they interview each other based on questions devised by the teacher and students together. Interviews are written up and/or put on video or audio tape. Interviews can include a portrait, clay statue, drama, song or poem about the partner.

Each child might just do one interview or over time interview several children. Each time the questions might be the same or different and the community building activity might be the same or different.

Community Building Activities

• Create a bulletin board displaying interviews with photos and/or other visual representations done.

- Partners do presentations for the rest of the class to share information learned about each other.

- *Name That Classmate!* (A game played like Twenty Questions:)

  Variation #1: Child has the name of a classmate taped to his/her back. Child asks yes/no questions based on interview information. Class answers thumbs up for "yes" and thumbs down for "no" until child can guess or reaches twenty questions.

  Variation #2: Teacher or child thinks of a classmate, whispers the name to one other person and then class asks yes/no questions based on interview information until name is guessed or twenty questions is reached. This can also be played with auto-biographical information.

  Variation #3: All students have the name of someone on their back. Everyone walks around asking and answering yes/no questions until someone guesses their name.

- Class Riddles and Bingo work well with this information too.

- *Partner Project:* Interview partners to find out ways they are alike and/or different and plan a project that would show this information. This could turn into a whole-class project, too.

Surveys

Children identify categories of personal and family characteristics and interests and carry out surveys to determine class statistics. These statistics can be graphed, compared and written about. Theme books can be created. "Our Favorite..." games can be played with this information, as mentioned in previous activities. As new surveys are thought of, class predictions can be made based on past survey information.

Community Building Art Projects

Puzzle Piece Mural

A large piece of mural paper is cut into puzzle piece shapes that fit together to make a complete sheet of paper. Each child has one piece of the puzzle on which they name and describe something that they are good at—that they can be counted on to do to help others in their class (good with math, good at fixing things, good with helping hurt feelings, good at tying shoes, etc.) These ideas can then be illustrated with a photograph or a drawing and all the pieces put together to make the "Class Caring Puzzle." These competencies are referred to and used often.

Hand Print or Foot Print Mural

Children put their hand print or foot print on a mural and alongside their print goes their name and a thought that child has about how she or he will help to make the classroom a friendly place—"Helping Hands for Friendliness" or "Steps to Being Friendly."

Friendship Quilt

Children create a quilt mural out of paper or cloth or a real quilt out of cloth. Each child decorates his own square or has her picture on it. The squares can be just a picture of the class together or each child can represent something that makes him special or something that makes the class special to her.

Children, Children Who Do You See?

This is wonderful to do with primary children. Read Bill Martin's *Brown Bear, Brown Bear What Do You See?* and then, based on that story, create a book that names every child in the class and has a photograph or portrait of that child.

Class Identity

Children can create a class name, class banner, class motto, class cheer, class symbol, class language, class song, class mascot, class handshake, class poem, class story, etc.

"New Friends" Activities

Several times a week children join together in partnerships in which the two children do not know each other very well or at all. These "new friends" times take place during familiar activities such as Morning Meeting (sitting next to a new friend), lunch time (eating with a new friend), choice or activity time (working on an activity with a new friend), game time (playing a board game or outdoor game with a new friend), etc. After each "new friends" time, some children are asked to share "A New Friends Fact" or something they have in common.

Facts that children wrote about themselves are accompanied by photographs the teacher took.

Conclusion

Spending the time to build community and learn about the children in all facets of their lives sets the foundation for a caring classroom where children feel competent and excited to meet the challenges of new learning. It also establishes the notion that learning can be fun! So be creative, let the children join in and enjoy those first few weeks!

Let's Do Lunch!

What a Teacher Can Do to Help a Class Have a Successful Lunch Experience

by Marlynn K. Clayton

ALL TOO OFTEN, the caring, cooperative, responsible, friendly behavior that is expected, practiced and seen in the classroom breaks down when the children hit the lunchroom.

To truly change the dynamics of the lunchroom environment, schools must address the issues through a school-wide effort involving all staff and an examination of the overall structures of the lunchroom. I highly recommend the educational and social value of "reforming" the lunchroom. Many schools involved in implementing Responsive Classroom practices school-wide have taken this pivotal step, and the positive effects are powerful.

My intention here is to suggest some strategies that the individual teacher can use with her own group of children regardless of the overall structure of lunch. These are steps which one teacher can take to make lunch a more positive experience. Certainly, these strategies could be used as well by all teachers in a school-wide lunchroom reform.

Lunch Has Purpose

In order for children to successfully meet behavior expectations and willingly work for a more positive lunchtime, teachers must first lay a foundation for meaningful purpose.

Preparing Children for Success

You can do this by discussing with your students the purpose of lunchtime. With this as a reference point of meaning, children can see the connection between their behavior and what they hope to achieve at lunch. Some of the kinds of questions you can ponder together in a classroom discussion about lunch include: *How will we take care of ourselves* and *each other so that we enjoy our lunch and our friends? and How does the cafeteria rule "Stay in your seats" help us to do this?*

In this way, children clearly understand the meaning behind the rules and structures of lunch and the expectations for their behavior. Ultimately these discussions lead to the final step of naming, modeling, role playing and practicing the specific behaviors that will prepare children for success.

Having lunch partners can provide a chance for all students to get to know each other.

Practice "Doing Lunch"

You can begin the practice of "doing lunch" in your classroom. For example, after a discussion about what you might say and do to be successful in the lunchroom, you can model lunchtime behaviors for your students. The children identify your actions, your words, possibly your thoughts and feelings and your affect.

Next, a few children model how they will act at lunch while the others notice their positive behaviors. Finally, you practice lunch as if you were all in the lunchroom. Continue this process until you have modeled and practiced all the important segments of lunchtime behavior from getting ready to go to lunch to returning from the cafeteria. Now, you can move to practicing in the cafeteria itself, not during lunch periods but at another time of the day. Whenever possible, enlist the help of the cafeteria workers as well.

Lunch Is Fun

When you set up structures and events that keep the quality of fun and enjoyment in lunchtime, children are better able to see a purpose to working cooperatively and managing some of the more challenging expectations. Here are some ideas that Responsive Classroom teachers are using.

Lunch Partners

The structure of "lunch partners" can have many positive effects on what happens during lunchtime. It eliminates a great deal of anxiety and competition around the issue of who sits next to whom and it gives children an opportunity to get to know all of their classmates.

Some structures and routines that have worked for Lunch Partners:

• Each day children are responsible for inviting or accepting an invitation from another classmate to be a lunch partner. This means they proceed through all the routines of lunch together from beginning to end. Each day of the week a child has a different partner.

An Important Consideration: In order to prepare children for this structure, a teacher must be sure to proactively address in discussion and then with modeling: Why might it be important to have different lunch partners? How does inviting and rejecting affect others? Can we say no to someone if we don't have a partner yet? What are our responsibilities to one another in being friendly classmates and lunch partners?

• Some days of the week can be pre-set as "new friends" day which means that children partner with someone whom they don't usually work or play with.

• Partners can be designated by random drawing or through

game or category identification (for example, matching puzzle pieces, boy-girl, children reading the same book...) The children can have great fun themselves establishing ways of identifying partners.

- Partners can be given the responsibility of giving each other a compliment at the end of lunch or at the "after-lunch" meeting, or share something new that the partners found they have in common.

- Partners can also be put into groups of four or six who then fill in a complete table. This group can be self-selecting or established by the teacher. A fun activity is for the group to try to figure out what category the teacher used to define their group.

Topics for Conversation

This is a positive way to build children's capacity and interest in having productive and socially skilled conversations with one another. Begin by exploring why we talk with friends and classmates and what makes a conversation or talk between people interesting and worthwhile.

From this discussion the class should be able to create a list of possible ingredients that would make a successful conversation. The children then can refer to this list as they practice and evaluate their skill of conversing.

With these ingredients in mind, the class can brainstorm a list of topics that might be interesting, worthwhile and/or fun for them to use as topics for talking during their lunchtimes. Some examples of topics: things to do on an overnight at a friend's house, favorite desserts, what makes a hero, favorite activities in the summer/winter...

Here is a sampling of activities that can be done with these topics:

- Have the children write the topics on separate cards and then put them all into a box. Periodically a topic can be drawn from the box in order to establish a "Conversation Topic for the Week." During that week it is the children's responsibility to have conversations about the topic with their lunch partner or group.

- Children can be asked to report back at the "after-lunch" meeting something that they learned about another person from their conversation.

- The results from a single Conversation Topic or a number of them can become the focus of a display that a class exhibits in the cafeteria—what we learned about each other from our lunchtime conversation. This can provide a model and stimulus for other classes to begin lunchtime conversations.

The results of Conversation Topics can also provide the content for some wonderful community-building books back in the classroom.

Eating is only one important component of lunch!
Students share a laugh together in the lunchroom.

Lunch Games

A simple but powerful strategy is to teach children some fun and appropriate games that can be used while waiting for lunch to be done. Again and again, we see children losing their self-control because of overly long "wait times."

Brainstorm a list, make sure everyone knows how to play, post the list and then each day before leaving the classroom remind children to pick a game that they will use if necessary.

Many of the activities that are used in Morning Meeting or on car trips are excellent for children to use in the cafeteria (Aunt Minerva, 20 Questions, Guess the Number, I See Something...).

Reflection and Evaluation

The "After-Lunch" Meeting

You can begin each afternoon with an "after-lunch" meeting in which you reflect on the events of lunch and celebrate success. You might choose one behavior each day and have children share how they're doing and what new strategies they've learned to be even more successful! Sharing compliments with each other about the specific ways they've noticed each other "being successful" is another way to build in a positive focus to the reflection. After sharing the success, you can also use this meeting to do some problem solving if some behaviors weren't successful.

Advocating for Cafeteria Reform

Preparing the children in your classroom for a peaceful and successful lunchtime is possible and can bring powerful results for your class. As you help your children to be successful at lunch, others will begin to notice that success. The first steps to reforming lunchtime practices and procedures lie with the individual teachers.

With a growing awareness among teachers, a school can begin to explore and address more broadly the overall cafeteria environment: use of space and furniture; the scheduling and class mixes; the routines and discipline; the supervision and signals; and the structures to build and practice social skills that will create a peaceful and enjoyable lunchtime experience for the entire school community.

Guided Discovery:
Teaching the Freedom to Explore

by Ruth S. Charney

*"To know enough about things is one
prerequisite for (having) wonderful ideas."*
(from Eleanor Duckworth's *The Having of Wonderful
Ideas and Other Essays on Teaching and Learning*)

IT IS MY PRACTICE to "open" the classroom gradually. Only some of the areas will be used the first week. Only some of the materials are out on the shelves. New things and new choices are introduced slowly. *Guided Discovery* is the process that I use to structure these first introductions to materials, routines, and areas of the classroom. The *Guided Discovery* protects children from the assault of a classroom that is too full of materials and choices at first and it provides deliberate teaching of work habits and social habits, skills and concepts. It is an opportunity to model, to role play and to represent a variety of outcomes. Our *Guided Discoveries* prompt and excite children to play, to explore, to communicate and to cooperate. The *Guided Discovery* that follows shows how this teaching structure unfolds.

The Box of Crayons

I often introduce a box of crayons, or perhaps a large set of markers with thirty-six-plus different colors during the first week of school. Deliberately, even with older groups, I start with a common, taken-for-granted, staple of the classroom. I want to extend the possibilities, as well as model a considered approach to the resources of our classroom.

I have covered the box of crayons with a wrapper. "Who can guess what I have? I'll give you a clue—it's something we frequently use in school." Quickly, this six-year-old group, feeling

37

Children are excited to try to name all the colors of crayons in this box.

and shaking the package, guesses correctly.

"Yes. It's a box of crayons. But how many . . . a few or a lot?" I ask.

"A lot," replies a chorus of voices.

"Well. What's a lot?" I question. I write down some of the numbers, enjoying the ideas of quantity that vary so with this age. One thousand, some say. Twenty-hundred is another possibility. Eighty-eight, a more precise fellow suggests.

"How will we find out?" I ask.

"Open it!" come the excited answers.

"Where does it tell us exactly how many?" I ask. As I hold up the box, different children try to locate and distinguish the numbers. Finding them easily, they are satisfied. And some will read them . . . but is it 46 or 64?

"Sixty-four crayons. That is a lot. Think now," I say, "are they all the same color? Are there sixty-four blue crayons? Sixty-four red crayons?" We take a quick inventory. Most are pretty sure that there are sixty-four different colors. "Do you think there might actually be sixty-four different colors?" Many nods. "Do you think you might be able to name 10 . . . 20?" Lots of nods.

Remember now, what we are exploring is a standard piece of equipment . . . not dazzling, not a jazzy new product! By the time I actually open the lid in order to display sixty-four different colors, there is considerable interest, even drama. "Let's see if you can figure out ten of these fancy colors. I wonder . . ." The children eagerly begin to name, first the obvious, and then silver, gold, turquoise. I put their inventory on a chart, locating the crayon with each given label. They name ten, then twenty, pleased with their own knowledge, excited by their own discoveries. Perhaps I will add one new color. "Here's a very fancy one . . . magenta, it says on its label. Can anyone guess what color magenta might be?" as I wiggle it in the box, but keep it hidden. Their guesses add to the final pleasure of discovery. . . . "It's sort of like reddish-purplish-pink," someone says. "It's like Kim's shirt." "Magenta . . . magenta," someone else sings.

Using the Crayons

The concept that there are shades of color, that magenta is a shade of red, would be an interesting one to develop in another lesson. Or it might have been a focus for an older group. Now, I move on to using the crayons. I explain that later in the morning there will be a drawing time. They will have a chance to use these special boxes of sixty-four crayons. "Where do you think we should keep them?"

"On the art shelf."

"Why would that be a good place?"

"Because you use them for drawing and art."

"Yes. They are things that artists use. How do you think artists take care of their crayons?" I ask. I show them that I have noticed how full the box is and how hard it can be to take out the crayons and find where to put them back. I demonstrate. "Should I just dump them all out, because I'm in a hurry?" I query.

"You gotta be careful," someone tells me.

"Show me how you would be careful," and a student comes up and gingerly extracts a single item. I make it 'tricky' and shake the box, challenging her to then replace it. She does. "How did you know to put it there?" I ask.

She smiles. "I could see."

"What could she see?" I ask the others. The rest of the class peers into the box, intrigued with this mystery. Others want to try, but I remind them that they will all have a chance when it's art (or choice time).

"I've noticed something else about these pretty crayons. I've noticed that they have a pretty sharp point."

"It's kind of roundish too," someone observes.

"What do you think will happen if I need to press down hard to make it dark?"

"It will break?"

"You shouldn't do it so hard."

"It gets flat."

"Suppose I want to make a dark sky and I press hard and it does break, but I want it sharp again. Does anyone know a way to sharpen a crayon? Can you sharpen crayons?"

"They get stuck a lot."

"They do get stuck in pencil sharpeners. Is there another way?" We might experiment with different types of crayon sharpeners at another meeting (a group of seven-year-olds once took off on a study of crayon sharpeners!), but for now I just introduce the tool.

Sharing the Crayons

Before finishing with the day's discovery lesson, I may need to talk about sharing. As one of the children finds space on our art shelf, I ask someone to count how many boxes we have in our class. There are six. Will that be enough for everyone? Suppose more than six children want to use them at the same time? Suppose the whole class wants to use them for drawing later? How will we do that? This may be a good time to introduce, or reinforce, behavior and language for sharing. Both are accomplished with modeling and role-playing. "If I want the black, do I say—gimme it! What should I say, remind me . . ." And I ask a child to demonstrate. I may propose other dilemmas such as what happens if the box is out of my reach or if we both need the same crayon at the same time . . . I find that children need to go through this, and gain comfort even when they have heard it before, and even when they are ten years old. To know that you can manage these courtesies and secure the management of a box of crayons is an important achievement. It is also important to how pleasant and proud we feel when our children are polite, kind and helpful to each other, to visitors or to us. It will break down for sixes. It will break down for eights.

Students feel good about knowing how to use materials—how to share the water bowl, what to do when the water looks muddy.

"Show me that you remember how to ask someone to pass over a marker," we say. "Remind me, what happens when . . . Who knows what to do if you have been waiting for the brown crayon for a long time? Is it okay to grab?"

As the children go to work with the crayons . . . or the math manipulatives. . . or their new readers . . . the role of the teacher, after the guided discovery, is to watch. To reinforce the discoveries notice the careful handling of the material, observe the social behaviors. "I see that you are trying both light and dark coloring." "I like the way you are passing the box around the table." "What nice words I hear. . ." "You found another new color. What other color do you think it's like? Would you like to add that to our chart so others can look for it?" And, of course, to remind and redirect, when children "forget."

Even older children gain from Guided Discovery lessons about familiar materials.

Guided Discovery Objectives

This process of a guided discovery opens the areas on the classroom and prepares the children for different aspects of the curriculum, at each age-level. It does not need to occur for every material or every potential activity. It is selective. I will present both familiar and new resources. One year, I started fourth graders with pencil sketching and new techniques for using the number two pencil. In any guided discovery lesson, there may be the following objectives:

1. To motivate by extending possibilities.

2. To give information and ideas to guide and deepen the understanding of materials and activities in the classroom.

3. To give instruction in the techniques and skills needed for effective use of tools and materials.

4. To establish a common language and vocabulary.

5. To share ideas and procedures for independent use of the material or area. (This may be prompted by the children who have invented alternatives or found new ideas.)

6. To teach or reinforce guidelines for social or cooperative uses.

7. To teach and reinforce care and clean-up routines.

Guided discovery lessons may introduce the entire class to an area of the program, such as how to use the library area or a "choice period." Or, they may be used to introduce and extend the use of specific materials and activities. They may establish routines for an entire group and/or for independent working. Certainly, as children develop their facilities with materials they become better able to manage them with minimal teacher supervision. Learning to work with care with a crayon or a microscope enhances its use and potential for individuals and groups.

The Responsive Classroom Environment
Some Thoughts on Display

by Marlynn K. Clayton

ROOM ENVIRONMENT is generally a component of teaching that we struggle with before school starts and are loathe to change once the children have arrived. However, not all changes in an environment require a drastic movement of furniture. It is important to reflect on the effectiveness of classroom design occasionally during the school year. With this in mind, I offer in this issue some thoughts on the critical element of display in the classroom.

Display in the Responsive Classroom reflects the creative, cognitive, individual and shared interests and accomplishments of the children. The content of display shows the ongoing collaboration in decision-making between the children and their teacher. At its best, display reveals the life of the classroom with beauty, clarity and simplicity.

Display is an extremely powerful tool in teaching. It is often not used appropriately nor recognized for its significance in teaching. The list of goals and purposes for display in the Responsive Classroom shows the wide range of its effects on all learning whether it be academic, social or aesthetic.

The practical and concrete applications of these goals are highlighted in the following photographs and descriptions. These ideas will be helpful to keep in mind while evaluating the effectiveness of display in your classroom. The displays pictured in these photographs are from Greenfield Center School classrooms.

General Bulletin Boards

Keep bulletin boards simple and uncluttered. Put up only what's necessary and most useful to the children at any one time. Use a plain color and texture for the background of any bulletin

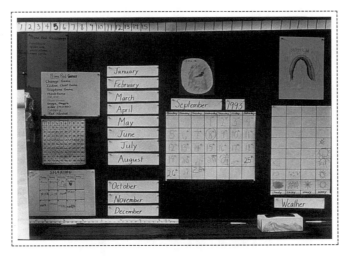

This bulletin board displays important information that children
refer to and interact with every day.

board. This K–1st grade board displays important information
that the children refer to and interact with every day:

- Ideas for Morning Meeting greetings and activities.

- The calendar and weather graph that each have an acetate
  overlay for children to write upon and easily re-use each month.

- Sharing sign-up for the week.

- An art gallery that highlights two or three "artists" each week.

- A number line that is added to each day.

- A number grid that is used constantly for reference in determining the date and the number line, as well as other counting
  and number activities.

- The bulletin board is at the children's eye level and makes a
  positive statement about the value placed upon teacher- and
  student-made materials.

Showing 3-D Articles

A place should be provided for children to exhibit three
dimensional work and "sharing articles." In this K–1st grade

This "Show Shelf" provides a place for children to display
three-dimensional work and "sharing articles."

classroom, all the materials necessary to create a beautiful and
informative display are easily accessible to all the children. The
3x5 cards, assorted crayons and wooden holders for the cards
are all arranged right on the shelf for easy use in labeling. This
creates the effect of a museum and with that comes a respectful
appreciation of the articles displayed.

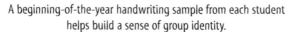

A beginning-of-the-year handwriting sample from each student
helps build a sense of group identity.

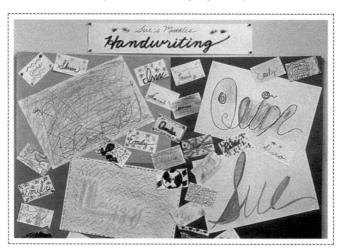

All-Class Displays

There should always be at least one display in the classroom that shows the effort and interest of every child. All-inclusive displays nurture that sense of equal ownership and an affirmation of equal value in the group. These displays, without grades or marks, will allow every child to feel valued regardless of their academic abilities.

Something as simple as displaying beginning of the year handwriting samples of each child's name has a powerful effect on creating community.

Photographs

In this 2nd grade classroom, a display of photographs of each child remains posted at eye level all year long. The photographs show each child engaged in a favorite accomplishment, such as riding a bike, playing the piano, or reading a book, which was demonstrated for the class in school. This display of photographs is a critical teaching tool used by the teacher and the children. It serves as a daily, concrete reminder to the children of their ability to learn skills as they cope with their struggles and successes in

Taken in the fall and displayed all year long, Prime Pride Day photographs show each child engaged in a favorite accomplishment.

learning and with their seven-year-old propensity for self doubt.

Other Displays

Other displays should highlight only a few children's work at a time. A simple, small heading provided by the teacher, or later by the children, can set the stage for rotation of children's work, each very beautifully presented. With lots of space to display, children learn how to arrange, label and accent different pieces of work. The next photos show a K–1st grade water color display, a 5th–6th grade mapping exercise and a 4th grade favorite book display. Children have learned how to create the effect of a frame by drawing a simple black line around the perimeter of their page.

Changing displays and their content regularly keeps the children's interest high in viewing and appreciating them, allows for many children to have opportunities to display even when display space is not adequate, and encourages a simplicity that truly highlights each child's work.

In the Responsive Classroom, children are given the opportunity to decide what work they wish to share. The need for these decisions leads to valuable discussions about defining appropriate criteria for choosing work for display, and thus provides the beginning foundation for reflection of one's own work and effort.

Environmental design both affects and defines the content and process of children's learning. By paying careful and continuous attention to display with Responsive Classroom goals in mind, teachers can create a classroom environment that stimulates and celebrates the learning of all children.

Here are examples of displays showcasing K–first grade watercolors, fifth–sixth grade maps, and fourth grade favorite book posters.

Reaching Out to Parents

by Chip Wood and Mary Beth Forton

A HEALTHY PARTNERSHIP between school and family is one of the most powerful unions teachers can help create. We have found that the energy we put into helping parents feel informed about and involved in their child's life at school yields enormous dividends.

Although there are many things a teacher can do throughout the school year to encourage a strong and productive relationship with parents, the beginning of the school year presents a natural opportunity to begin this process. It is a time when both teachers and parents are focused on hopes for their children's year. In this article, we'll outline methods we find effective for initiating a parent-teacher partnership based on cooperation and trust.

The First Contact

The first step is to reach out to parents as soon as possible. Rather than waiting until November, scheduling the first parent-teacher conference during the early weeks of school helps teachers to develop a solid relationship with parents. Not only is the information exchanged at such a conference helpful, but it also creates a positive context which makes it easier to communicate about issues and problems that arise during the year.

Inviting Parent Input

A powerful way to open the dialogue with parents is to begin the conference by asking "What do you think is most important for your child to learn this year?" Not only does this question engage the parents immediately in a meaningful way, but it sets a tone of collaboration, and the answers give us important insights into our new students.

50

Some teachers send a letter home prior to this meeting to give parents time to think about their goal for their child (see sample letter). The parents' response in the conference then provides a point of interest with which to start this conversation between parents and teacher.

Responding to Parent Goals

"I'm worried about his math skills," shares Martin's father. "Shouldn't he know his times tables by now?" As we listen to his concern and note the goal, we might also follow this up by telling him what our plans are for this year's math program.

At this initial conference we use a form which both parent and teacher can keep to document the goal. This form serves as our reminder and assures parents that we have heard and understood their goal. It is an important reference as we monitor the work of the child in this area and we refer to this goal in future communications with parents and on report cards.

To give the process meaning and purpose, we let parents know from the start that we plan to document progress in the goal area. We want them to know that we really care about their goal and will be paying attention to it throughout the year. We try to save tangible evidence that shows the child's progress in this area, evidence that we can show to parents and include in a child's portfolio, or simply share with child and parent as a measure of growth.

Although many parent goals focus on academic progress, some parents wonder about social goals. "I think Robin is doing just fine with her school work," a parent says, "but what I'd really like her to do this year is to make some friends."

If we see the issue named as one that we're able and willing to work on with the child, we ask parents at this point if this is the area they'd like us to focus on with their child for the year. In this example where the goal involves social skills, documentation of growth may include photographs of the child working or playing with a friend, a story the child wrote about a friend, or teacher-written observations of the child in social situations.

Sample Parent Conference Letter

Dear Parents,

This year we will be doing our parent-teacher conferences differently than we have in the past. I feel very excited about these changes.

First of all, we will hold our first conference much earlier in the school year. This will allow teachers to get to know parents sooner and to learn more about our students. I believe this will strengthen the connection and greatly improve the communications between home and school.

At this first conference, I will be asking you to talk about your hopes for your child's school year. Specifically, I would like to know what you think is most important for your child to learn in school this year. Please choose one goal which you would like us to focus on. I will be paying careful attention to this goal and documenting growth in this area. At mid-year, we'll evaluate your child's progress in this area and decide whether to continue with this goal or, if the goal is accomplished, to choose another.

During this first conference, I will also share with you my plans and goals for this school year and answer any questions you may have. I am looking forward to working together with you to make this a wonderful year of learning for your child.

Sincerely,

Sharing Your Hopes and Goals

After the parent goal has been established and discussed, it is a good time to talk about our hopes and goals for the class and the student this year. The process of discussing each other's goals for the year allows teachers and parents to think aloud together and to understand each other's points of view. Sharing information is a vital part of the foundation upon which parents' investment and involvement will be built.

While most parents bring a lifetime of knowledge about their children to the conference, we usually have much less. Yet it is important to feel that we really know a child well enough to formulate a goal for her. Sometimes a prior year's records inform us, or a chat with last year's teacher. When we do get information about the child from previous teachers, we often ask parents about their perceptions. For example, past teachers may have commented that a child is easily distracted and can't concentrate on work. We've found it helpful to raise the issue with parents before a problem has developed in this year's classroom and teachers and parents feel strained or defensive. It can be illuminating to find out what the parents' thoughts are. Do they have a different perception? Do they know of some strategies that could be helpful to their child and teacher? Are they looking for help with this issue?

Of course, these conferences will not always run smoothly. Some parents don't show up or respond to our letters. We must leave the door open to these parents, perhaps sending them a follow-up letter telling them we missed them; letting them know what our goals are for their child or the class, inviting them to add their own goal either through a note or phone conversation.

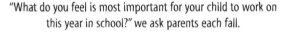

"What do you feel is most important for your child to work on this year in school?" we ask parents each fall.

Handling Unrealistic Goals

Occasionally we encounter parents who choose a goal which we know is unrealistic for their child. At this point in the year, we try to acknowledge the positive in the goal. We try not to contest it or to come across as the expert which may put the parents

---

From *Teaching Children to Care*
(by Ruth Sidney Charney, published by NEFC)

Our school schedules a pre-school and late-fall conference. At the first conference, parents are asked to think about their priorities for their child. "What do you feel is most important for your child to work on this year in school?" Often the parents share compelling insights, pertinent history, lingering anxieties and deep aspirations. We find out about children's interests, habits, attitudes and struggles.

We are all sometimes afraid for our children, fearful that lacking certain accomplishments, they will not hold their own in the world. These worries and hopes can produce a flood of demands on top of existing teaching prescriptions which assess and measure numerous discrete skills. If we are not careful, we start the year preparing for a marathon. When we ask ourselves and parents, "What is most important?" we intend to shorten the list and highlight a plan. The more we identify a focus, the better able we are to devote attention and effort to a course of improvement. And the more tangible successes children experience, and parents and teachers witness, the more pride and hope we create.

Children are responsive to the concerns and expectations issued by their parents and teachers. "I don't like the math we are doing right now," explained Tyrone, "but I know it's important for me." He "knows" because his parents have emphasized his need to improve his accuracy and proficiency with operations. He cares, not because the material provides intrinsic satisfaction or interest, but because of his authentic desire to please.

---

on the defensive. We remind ourselves that the purpose of this conference is to understand and communicate, to establish a warm and working relationship with the parent in which they feel invested in their child's school year.

So, for instance, when the parents of a first-grader tell us that they want their child to be able to read Hardy Boys books by December, we might respond by acknowledging the parents' interest in their child's reading progress and by talking about our reading program this year. The goal can be paraphrased on the form as "Parent wants Jamie to get better at reading."

Parents may change their goals as the year progresses. Some goals may be accomplished in two months; some may take two years. At some point close to the middle of the year (at our next conference or in a letter attached to the mid-year report card), we like to check in with parents by asking them "How do you think your child is doing in meeting the goal?" and "Has your goal for your child changed?" The feedback we receive gives us valuable information and lets us know whether our perception of a child matches the parent's perception.

Family Inventory

In addition to this September parent conference, we like to send out a Family Inventory at the beginning of

As the year progresses, there are many ways for teachers and administrators to continue to build a strong relationship between home and school. The book, *At Home in Our Schools: A Guide to Schoolwide Activities That Build Community* published by Developmental Studies Center (available from NEFC), offers many specific ideas and guidance for planning activities throughout the school year which will help all parents feel welcome at school.

Some examples include:

Family Heritage Museum

Family Projects Fair

Family Read-Aloud

Family Science Night

Family Film Night

the school year as a way to establish a connection with families and to welcome parents and grandparents into the classroom.

In this inventory, parents and grandparents are asked if they would be willing to volunteer some of their time in the classroom. The inventory asks them to list any special talents, skills, interests or cultural traditions which they would be willing to share. This offers a way to learn about our students' families, to help parents and grandparents feel welcome, and to bring rich resources into the curriculum.

Parents as partners in the education of their child widen the potential for the growth of every child. Inventories, conferences and goal-setting all help enlist parents and let parents know that we, as teachers, wish their help. When parents feel this welcome into their child's classroom, warm and collaborative teacher-parent relationships are possible and form a rich foundation for work with the child during the year.

When Parents Visit The Classroom

by Marlynn K. Clayton

P ROVIDING MANY AND VARIED OPPORTUNITIES for parents
to visit and be involved in classrooms is an important part of a
teacher's job. Some careful planning and preparation to set up
structures for parents' involvement will help make it a positive
experience for all involved—children, parents and the teacher.

Parent visits and classroom involvement are shaped by five
goals. These goals are:

1. To make parents feel warmly welcomed and included in the
   classroom and school community.

2. To help parents understand how and what their children are
   learning and why this learning and approach are important
   in terms of their children's growth.

3. To involve parents in classroom experiences and events
   which strengthen the parent/child relationship.

4. To give parents opportunities to see modeled some teaching and management strategies used in the classroom.

5. To have parent involvement occur within the normal structures of the established learning environment. All adults and
   children are expected to work and interact with mutual
   respect, care and interest, following the agreed-upon rules
   of the room.

These tips will share some of the ways Responsive Classroom
teachers meet these goals for parents' visits in their classrooms—
during one-to-one conferences; during occasional, often sponta-
neous visits; and when parents come to be regular or planned
classroom helpers.

One-to-One Conferences

• When requesting a conference, give parents an outline of the agenda and specifically mention a positive experience their child has had that you want to share in more detail. This is especially important to do with parents who themselves are threatened by school or whose experience in conferring about their child has often been around negative issues.

- Try to offer a variety of conference times, including some evenings, so that parents can more easily come. Encourage your school to offer child care for young students and their siblings. If that is not possible, have a corner of the room set up with quiet activity materials that will occupy them.

- Meet and warmly greet parents at the door of your classroom. This sets a comfortable tone as you bring them into the conference.

- Meet at a table where each member of the conference can feel equal. Using a teacher's desk can make this difficult.

- Try to begin every conference in such a way that the parent feels your support and sees you as an ally. You might share a recent accomplishment or an interesting piece of work. You might ask a question prompting the parent to think about the child in a positive way, such as "Tell me a way you've seen your child grow in the last few months."

- Structure the conference in ways that will maximize the information you gather and that will make parents aware of your genuine interest in their perspective.

Ask open-ended questions to get parents talking about their perspective. (What do you hope your child will learn in school this year? How does your child play with friends at home? What kind of things are easy/hard for your child to do at home?)

Paraphrase and highlight main points of parents' responses to show that you are hearing their perspective.

Focus on the dialogue between you and parents rather than solely on finding "a solution." Sometimes much is accomplished by the discussion itself, and often taking a week or so of "thinking and observing time" before meeting again can be very positive.

- Set up a regular time when parents may call to talk or ask questions that don't necessarily require a conference. Formalizing and announcing this to parents ("I'll be available by phone Tuesday evenings from 7–8:30") makes parents feel more comfortable about doing it. Make sure, however, that parents understand that they may approach you anytime with an urgent question or concern.

Parents and families enjoyed visiting this display which featured a piece of work from every student in the school.

Occasional and/or Spontaneous Visits

- Send home a general invitation to parents to visit, listing good visiting times and classroom events. This invitation can include time parameters, the goal of the event, and a focus for the parent, when such information is pertinent.

Times that work well in many classrooms are:

Morning Meeting
Lunch (in general or on specific days such as "Grandparents' Lunch")
Writing time
All-School Meeting (a time when the whole school gets together to share singing, works finished or in progress, news of school events)

- Children can write invitations to their parent/family member asking them to visit either for a particular event or for general visiting.

- Sending home a brief set of Visiting Guidelines along with a general invitation is helpful. These guidelines might look something like this:

General Guidelines for Visiting

1. Our goal is for children to be independent workers who support one another by working cooperatively and with self-control. To encourage this, please:

   Interact with children by asking them to tell you about their work or what they're doing.

   Give help only when a child asks for help.

   Before giving help, please first ask children what they have done to try and figure out the problem and whether they have asked a friend for help.

   Please follow the rules of our classroom, particularly the signals we use. A bell ringing means "Freeze" and "Quiet." A raised hand means "Quiet. Listen."

2. If you have questions or concerns about anything you see happen in the classroom during your visit, please check in with me about it before you leave. Your perceptions bring information that is helpful to me, and I want to hear your questions and concerns. This will help us work as a team in the classroom.

3. When we talk with children, our goal is to help them know the skills they're using, the learning they've done and the appropriate behavior to use. For example:
   I notice you are cooperating with your partners.
   I see that you did all the problems!
   When you figured out that science problem you had to use lots of new skills.

4. Your handout might list guidelines for specific events of the day, such as Morning Meeting Guidelines.

Please join in our circle.
Feel free to participate as a member of our classroom.
Allow children to do their jobs independently as usual.

A parent gets to read her young author's latest book
during a classroom visit.

When Parents are Regular Classroom Helpers

Parents really like to know specific ways that they can help. Many teachers provide a list of some ways they welcome help and collect names of interested parents at the beginning of the year.

Holding a training meeting to prepare your group of helpers can help things run smoothly. You might provide a written list of responsibilities for each specific job, i.e. reading to children or helping in art.

Some general information about your approach to working with children is useful for helpers.

For example, let them know that you want children to do the work. Their role is to enable, to watch and encourage the children.

Giving models for conversation with children about their work is valuable. *"Tell me about your drawing, Eric."*

Let parents know what management signals the class is accustomed to, such as bell-ringing or hand-raising. Make sure they feel free to call upon the teacher when a simple reminder or redirection doesn't improve any problematic behaviors.

Though creating structures for parent involvement requires an initial investment of time and energy, those structures, once in place, mostly sustain themselves. Having children see their parents as respected and visible participants in their school life makes a powerful statement. And the regular presence of parents in the classroom can bring a diversity of style and a richness of experience that no one teacher alone can provide.

About the Authors

Marlynn K. Clayton, co-founder of Northeast Foundation for Children, is currently NEFC's director of Professional Development. She has run her own preschool, taught in primary grades, and has worked with teachers nationwide through workshops and consulting. She created the videotape, *Places to Start: Implementing the Developmental Classroom* and co-authored *A Notebook for Teachers*.

Mary Beth Forton has taught in grades kindergarten through eight, has run a summer camp for elementary school children and has worked with children with special needs. She currently works in the Publishing Division at Northeast Foundation for Children.

Ruth Sidney Charney, author of *Teaching Children to Care* and *Habits of Goodness: Case Studies in the Social Curriculum*, has taught grades kindergarten through eight and has worked as a teacher educator as well. Ruth is a co-founder of Northeast Foundation for Children and currently teaches grades seven and eight.

Chip Wood, author of *Yardsticks: Children in the Classroom Ages 4–14*, is a co-founder of Northeast Foundation for Children. He has worked for over 25 years as a classroom teacher, teaching principal and teacher educator. Currently he directs NEFC's Consulting Teachers.

Additional Teacher Resources from
Northeast Foundation for Children

Responsive Classroom: A Newsletter for Teachers

Published three times a year, this newsletter is full of practical information for educators. A free subscription is available by contacting NEFC.

Habits of Goodness: Case Studies in the Social Curriculum
by Ruth Sidney Charney

Six elementary school teachers study problems from their class-rooms concerning the social curriculum. 196 pages

Teaching Children to Care: Management in the Responsive Classroom
by Ruth Sidney Charney

Offers practical approaches for bringing the practice of caring into K–8 classrooms. 309 pages

Yardsticks: Children in the Classroom, Ages 4-14
by Chip Wood

User-friendly guidebook with clear and concise descriptions of devel-opmental stages of children. 228 pages

On Their Side: Helping Children Take Charge of Their Learning
by Bob Strachota

An elementary school teacher shares strategies for helping children invest in their learning. 160 pages

A Notebook for Teachers: Making Changes in the Elementary Curriculum
by Northeast Foundation for Children Staff

Ideas for creating a developmentally appropriate classroom curriculum and environment for 5, 6 and 7 year olds. 79 pages

Places to Start: Implementing the Developmental Classroom
by Marlynn K. Clayton

This video offers a wealth of ideas for creating active and caring class-room communities, K–3. 90 minutes

For Ordering Information

NEFC Publishing Division
71 Montague City Road
Greenfield, MA 01301

PHONE: 800-360-6332 ext. 2
FAX: 413-772-2097
E-MAIL: nefc@crocker.com